DON'T
LET THE LIGHT
GO OUT

A STORY OF TRUE LOVE, INSECURITIES, LOSS,
AND ACCEPTANCE

Shaun Anthony Marshall

Dedicated .to Anthony and Rob

Very proud and honoured to have you both in my life.

ABOUT THE AUTHOR

"In a world often governed by reason, he is a soul led by heart. A successful businessman, an artist of profound expression, a devoted husband and father, and a lover of life's endless possibilities, he is a man who walks the delicate line between reality and dreams.

His journey, paved with triumphs and heartbreaks, has forged within him an unshakable belief that with faith, all things are possible. Through the written word, he bares his soul—raw, unfiltered, and unapologetically human. His poetry and prose are not mere ink on paper; they are fragments of a heart that has loved deeply, lost painfully, and dared to hope once more.

Each piece within this collection serves as a window into his soul, offering readers not only a glimpse of his emotional depths but an invitation to reflect on their own. For those who have loved and lost, for those who seek healing through words, and for those who still believe in the power of hope—his work awaits you.

Dare to feel.

Dare to heal.

Dare to believe that, perhaps, love was never lost... merely waiting to be found."

TABLE OF CONTENTS

CHAPTER 1

Schools Out!

My school years at boarding school started when I was 9 years old. It was an old mansion house. My time at Hurn Court School was a blur of trying to survive in a system that did not understand me.

I suffer from dyslexia—not being able to read, write, or spell was my silent battle, my embarrassment, and my shame. I carried it with me every day and, to some extent, still do.

I was left at school incredibly early, four to five hours early, so there were only a few kids there. I was just left. Some older boy was made to show me around the school until everyone arrived.

It was quite scary being away from home. Eventually, I got used to the routine. Boarding school is all about routine.

At every lesson change, a big bell was rung! It was an old-school thing.

I ran away twice; I had no idea where I was going. It was just a shoutout to be noticed. I got detention instead!

At half term, I would rather go to a friend's home than to my family home. I never knew anyone there, and I would have just been alone again.

I only ever came home at the end of the school term—in the summer and Christmas holidays. Eight weeks of misery in unfamiliar surroundings.

We moved around the country a lot as my dad was in the RAF, so I would often come home to a new, strange town.

I would rather be at school, at least I knew people there.

I got the cane, slipper, or detention many times, sometime a wack across the knuckles with a blackboard rubber. That was the punishment for not keeping to the rules in those days.

I was not a naughty kid, but I always seemed to be the one to get caught! Teachers labeled me as 'thick' and 'unteachable,' telling me I would never amount to anything. Those words stuck with me, sinking deep into my bones.

But more than the words, I used to think that because a teacher said it, it must have been-true!

I can remember most times when I came home from school on holidays, and I had to have extra tests (with special bricks, shapes, and letters) to find out what was wrong with me. Mum and Dad never said much about the tests or what they were looking for.

In my young life at school, there was the absence of anything loving, something caring–something every child should have.

I never got a hug, and if I did, it was not often.

Never got kissed on the lips, or very rarely.

Never felt a kiss on my forehead.

Never heard someone say, "You did well!" or "Well done!"

It felt like no one liked me or particularly cared.

I had always been invisible, it seems, to the people I thought loved me.

I was never good enough.

I had nothing like a family.

To this day, it is all I have ever wanted. A family of my own, a family that would not leave me.

CHAPTER 2

Sports

Sports became my escape.

The track, the rugby pitch—those were the only places where the noise in my head went quiet.

I became the first team's rugby captain. We were a good team.

I had a few friends in the team, Paul Sheppard, the hooker, and a great chap called Lewis Benn (he was fast).

I was on the wing as I was also quick.

We toured Paris, France, and parts of Wales.

I also ran the 1500 metres, and won the team cup, eventually I ran for the county team "Hampshire"

Cross country running was also one of my strengths, setting at the time, the schools fastest under 15s race time.

I wasn't just running against other people as much as I was running from the feeling that I was useless.

Now, I race go-karts.

I have raced all over the UK, Silverstone, Rye House, Milton Keynes, and many other tracks. Nowadays, I race on my brother's track.

My brother, Rob, is an amazing man. He's had his problems but now runs one of the best racetracks in the Canaries.

We are remarkably similar, but unlike me, he seems in control of his life and very calm—nothing fazes him, unlike me. He is very measured; I am all over the place, not listening, not understanding.

Nowadays, I chase for lap times, and the win, the adrenaline, the focus, it only matters for a second, and then, it is gone. But in that second, I feel free. I feel like I can do anything, and my head is surprisingly quiet (it's normal for me to be talking so fast in my head).

Often, I do not know what do do or say. It is usually the wrong thing, but karting was a great place to find my peace. I was on a mission to be the fastest, the winner at something—anything so people would see me.

I had a major kart accident when I was racing in London—two punctured lungs and damage to my neck and spine. It was touch and go if I would survive.

My brother was informed. Luckily, my wife rushed down to the hospital in London to be with me. I remember the drive home to Norfolk—how every bump in the road hurt like hell. It took us hours to get home.

I was off work for ten long weeks and then sent back to the hospital with further complications.

CHAPTER 3

College Years

College was chaos. I had no direction and few choices: catering, motor engineering, resitting my exams, or hairdressing. Of all the things, I picked hairdressing, but it felt right. The fact was I had no other choice, so I had to do it, or in my mind I would be a complete failure.

As you can imagine, I was not prepared to step into a class of thirty-five girls after leaving an all-boys school. It was daunting.

It was at college that I met David. David was in my class, and he was a Spanish American. He had it all, the good looks, was wealthy, a snappy dresser, and very confident. He had his own car, his own apartment, and his life was all figured out. His father was very wealthy and wanted David to become something, anything. All David wanted was to have fun!

He became my guide with the girls; he taught me so much. He never had his heart in hairdressing. I think he was there to keep his father happy, but David was there to play and have fun with the girls.

College was exciting. I settled and grew to like it. I liked hair and was very curious to find out everything I could.

If you know me, I talk a lot. Hairdressers need to have the skill of chatting, and it is my greatest skill: talking!

I now know it was a way to hide my insecurities.

We had to share clients in class as there were never enough models, and the models were always the same ones each week, with only three hairs on their heads!

I hated sharing a client. I wanted to see what I could accomplish myself, so as you can imagine, I was never satisfied. But I knew I was getting good at it.

I met Lester then. Lester was a top salon owner and a college teacher in the Kings Lynn area. He ran the top advanced class in the evenings at college. I was not allowed to attend his class because I was seen not to be good enough.

Eventually, I plucked up the courage and snuck into his classes, not to cheat the system—just to prove that I had something special to offer.

Lester was impressed that I had the courage to attend his class, and as it turned out, at the end of the two-year course, I was one of the top students.

Even then, I was into the technical way of cutting hair. A skill of how to build a shape, to bring something into existence that did not exist and make it a reality.

I was amazed I could do it, and I am still cutting hair today. All the other students in my class either did not bother as much or stopped a good few years ago.

Lester saw something in me. He gave me a job. I had won. I had been seen!

My real training began in London, as that is where the top salons are. The excitement of London was like nothing I had experienced before. I was in a trance-like state every time I attended a cutting course.

I trained in London, in the Mayfair and Soho area, and spent all my money and most holidays at Toni & Guy, Videl Sassoon, and the Jingles academies.

I was getting good.

But I had no one to share it with.

No one to tell me that they were proud. Whether I was proud or not, I just knew I could do this, and I loved it.

I was lucky that I became good friends with Anthony and Bruno Mascolo, two of the four brothers who created Toni & Guy.

My son was named after Anthony, and one of my dogs after Bruno.

CHAPTER 4

Love and Mistakes

I got married and divorced twice.

My first marriage lasted around eighteen months. It was a bit strained from the beginning. Now, as I look back, I see that she, too, was seeking approval from her parents.

We had a son. I always wanted to be a part of something, but at the time, I was not expecting a baby–I must be honest.

I was busy trying to build my business; it was the only thing no one could take away from me, or so I thought!

I was excited. I had a boy. My boy. It was strange to think of myself as a father! But it was equally amazing.

Anthony, my son, is now thirty-two. He became my constant. He has grown into a strong, clever man. He works with computers. Even though he tells me what he does, I still have no clue what he is talking about.

He gives me lots of advice. I look at him and wonder how someone so young understands things about my issues (ADHD) and emotions that I never did.

I never noticed, especially the problems within me. I thought I was normal!

When I chat with him, I always feel uplifted; he always has the knack to make me feel better. He is rich in his heart and, like me, tries to help other people.

I am so immensely proud of him. I'm so happy that now we spend excellent quality time together.

Quite often, her mum and dad made it quite difficult for me to build a relationship with Anthony. I was not allowed to see him as often as I would have liked, and even then, the times and days were often changed at the last minute to suit their needs, never mine.

Anthony was so young that it was easy for them to tempt him to do something with them. It would have always been a better option than what his dad was offering.

We have managed over the years to become remarkably close and love each other deeply. It's a blessing I got so lucky with him.

My second marriage went a similar way, but she was different.

I first saw her walking down the road with a cut-out poster of Prince. Now, I had to know more. She was always doing something crazy, all sorts of different stuff, very arty. I liked that she had lots of interest and was just a genuinely nice person. We got on great and had many adventures. Our relationship lasted about ten years, but we were only married for two.

I loved her very much; it was a shame that she got away.

I do not think I noticed it, but my mother, it seemed, did not want me to be happy. She meddled in every single relationship—and I mean every relationship.

My mother had a hand in my first and second marriages, in fact, even with my girlfriends.

Sticking the knife into both and belittling them all. That was never good. And, of course, wife no. 2 left me.

Was it my behavior? Or was it my mum's interference?

I did not see just how much damage had already been done. I was too busy to see—or probably to notice.

I remember once I was home from school, and my mum caught me smoking. She made me stand on the staircase as I was tall. She horsewhipped me twice on the back of my legs, and two huge welts appeared on my legs.

I can still feel the welts, and I remember it as if it were yesterday. I smiled at her and never said a word or cried.

I then had another smoke. It hurt, really hurt.

My mum never seemed that happy with me. As if I had not met her expectations. She always expected a lot from me. I never really wanted to visit her, but of course, being the dutiful son, I gave in and took her for coffee or took her out shopping.

She was an unhappy lady, and with all her illnesses and loneliness, I could understand.

Unfortunately, Mum had diabetes, was losing her eyesight, and had a list of other ailments, so I cannot really blame her for being unhappy.

I could have been a much better son.

Mum and Dad are no longer with us; they have passed away.

I was sad but never cried.

CHAPTER 5

Paradise

My salon was one of the best in the area. I managed to build three salons in total. The first one I opened at nineteen years old. I was not sure quite what I was doing, but slowly, it grew to become successful. Six years later, I opened another and then a training salon.

Eventually, I ended up with only one salon. I could focus on one salon much better. I could not cope well with trying to run three salons. I was creative and not as interested in the business side, but even so, I made sure we were financially strong.

All my energy went into my salon. I was lucky it was super successful. I called being in the salon being in paradise.

I had the pleasure of having an apprentice called Lucy. She was the last stylist I had the privilege to help train. So, I have always been immensely proud of her, and she is now a very accomplished stylist. Even with a big age gap, we have remained good friends.

Many years later, I got arthritis in my shoulder and arm—because of many years of doing the same movements—and repetitive strain syndrome. I am sure racing accidents did not help either.

I am glad to say the doctors sorted it out, but I had to slow down.

My body and arms hurt. After all the years of blow-drying, my shoulders were messed up. I had an operation to remove some bone, and eventually, it all was ok, but my strong arm was left very weak and very sore with a little tremble.

I was persuaded and decided to take early retirement and go to live abroad and try to chill out and be with my brother, Rob.

Rob had moved abroad; he had opened a racetrack, so I decided I would go and join him. I knew it was not going to be easy as I loved my job and the business that I had spent 40+ years building.

Over the years, my salons had some of the best stylists. We built a fantastic reputation—we were busy, had a full client list, and, best of all, I got to focus on my favourite subject of all: recommending and selling haircare products. We sold a lot of products. All my hard work and dreams had come true.

Unfortunately, within a few months, two girls left the salon to build their own dreams. I really had no hard feelings; I just hoped they would succeed, and I hoped my training would help them become successful.

I had to come back to the UK to try and save my salon, but unfortunately, I could not. So, eventually, I had to start the process of closing it down.

CHAPTER 6

Photography, My Passion

Picture this:

I found photography.

But only on my iPhone, not a real camera.

I am not a photographer, but amazingly, I took some beautiful pictures. I managed to sell quite a few; people liked them and said I had a great eye for them. To me, they were just pictures.

I was still thinking I was not good enough. It was just me alone, walking on the beach or the woods with my dog, and something would capture my eye—the colour, the sound, the shape—and I would take the photo in that moment, no hesitation.

The local paper and even the local council asked to use two of my pictures. I was shocked that they thought they were good enough, but of course, I said yes.

I took lots of pictures.

I could see what others did not see or notice. My pictures were always full of colour, taken at strange angles, unusual shapes, and without any filters. It was just what I saw, what I felt at that moment.

My pictures were of trees, the wild sea, unusual buildings, and now people. I like the woodland and the beach best, it was always different every time I visited.

It was how I saw the world, always full of colour, bright and shiny, and never gray or dull; it is how I see life,

I always look to find the good!

Again, people made nice comments, even suggesting I should put them in art shows, but of course, I have not had the courage to do that yet. To me, they are just pictures.

My last set of pictures was of couples walking hand in hand on the beach or the prom.

Now when I look back at them subconsciously, I realise that is what I wanted: someone special (Kerry) to hold on to. It is what I always wanted.

I then started to put music in my pictures, trying to convey my feelings in that moment.

I hoped someone would notice my reels; it was my cry for help because that is what it was: a cry to anyone who was looking, a cry to my girlfriend. I knew her daughter followed me, so I hoped she would see them and show her mum.

I do not think she ever did.

CHAPTER 7

Bad Thoughts

Suicide.

It is always digging away at me. It crossed my mind many times, even a few days ago. I think it has always been there in my inside voice.

I do not know how to get out of this cycle. Naturally, I am an incredibly positive person, but it only takes a problem that I cannot see a way through or cannot get over, and the thoughts are back.

It has always been there at the back of my mind.

I had a girlfriend who committed suicide. She was frightened of getting old.

She was only forty-seven at the time, and she was lovely and kind, so full of life.

She felt that she needed Botox, lip fillers, an eye lift—in fact, any treatment you can think of. She would go anywhere to get it done, no matter what the cost.

Of all people, she did not need any of it, but in her mind, she was terrified of looking and getting old.

We all have our demons.

CHAPTER 8

Everyday People

I need people around me; I need that special person with me.

Kerry was my special person.

I'm hopeless without people.

People give me power and give me strength. I love being with people. I spent my whole professional life being around people.

I now realise that I was alone on the island—some days, some weeks, not speaking to anyone apart from "Ola." With the language barrier, it was driving me insane.

As I mentioned before, I had moved abroad, but within a few weeks, some of my team left my salon.

I tried to salvage what I could on the phone every day with the remaining team, but it was not going to work, so I had to come back to the UK to close it down.

Seeing my salon shut its doors after some forty years was brutal and sad, but it had to happen.

I told you before, everyone leaves me.

I was back in the UK; it was very cold, but something amazing was about to happen.

CHAPTER 9

The Love I Lost

I saw her walking in the park.

I was about to go back abroad for a week's holiday, but luckily, I got her number. She was a tall, long-legged woman with wild hair, wearing a big bobble hat, who, even in the gloom of a British winter morning, looked lovely.

She was curious about me. I could tell.

We started texting. We texted every day, like new lovers do. I could not wait to get back home. I was showing her pictures of my home and the island, and she liked it and was growing to like me.

I felt so lucky to have found her. She was just so nice, a little reserved, kinda classy, but carefree. I liked her. She was not my normal type.

When I came back, we started a relationship. As always, at the beginning, it was fantastic.

I was full of stories, which I think she found funny. She said she liked my humour and found my stories interesting.

Like most men, some were just made up to try to impress her, and I wanted to impress this woman. She was a catch.

I liked her from the start. She was strong, funny, thoughtful, and, in my eyes, beautiful.

A tall blonde, what could go wrong?

She always had a quietness.

We had a few meals out. I remember Valentine's evening. It was great. I was the proudest man in the pub, with the prettiest girl in the place. We talked all evening, and I was so nervous. I hoped it didn't show.

Most nights, I would invent some story about what I was cooking that evening. I am no cook, and my cooking was pretend. I faked it, but I wanted her there, so any excuse to cook for her and just to spend more time together. She came around most nights. It was great, and we had a lot of fun.

Little did I know then that she was and is an amazing cook. She must have thought I was an idiot with all my showing off about my kitchen skills.

She could make anything: cakes, sweets, etc. We made soda bread; it seemed so easy when she showed me the process.

We talked, cuddled, and did all the stuff new couples do. It was lovely; she was not like the other girls I had met before—very respectful and caring.

We were together for over six months, talking every day. I had so much to share, so many stories and experiences to share with her, the pyramids, America, history, and my travels. She even started to get interested in and like Formula One. I'm a big Lewis Hamilton fan, so she wanted to know all about him. You name it, everything I wanted to share with her. Poor girl.

I grew close to her quite quickly. I did not tell her how much I liked her, just in case she freaked out. I know she liked me a lot, but to be on the safe side, I said nothing.

Straight away, I knew she was the girl for me. She showed me so much care; it was lovely—but equally scary. I was not used to that kind of attention. But I loved it.

Then, one night, I finally said it: *'I love you.'* And I really did!

Later that week, she said it back to me.

As you can imagine, I was in heaven.

We started dreaming and planning a life together.

We started to make plans for a new adventure abroad. She quickly sold her house and gave up her job. She was about to make a big decision.

I made sure it was her decision, her choice. I never pushed her into anything, as it was such a big step.

She was ready to take the leap of faith with me. That was all I needed—the confidence to do it again with someone who loved me.

From there, I thought I could build us both a new exciting future. If you remember, my first attempt to live abroad was a failure.

I returned to the island, getting the house ready. She was living in our house in the UK.

I told her, "This is your home until you do not want us anymore!"

Even then, I would not have ever kicked her out.

I kept telling her, "What is mine is yours," and I meant it.

I could understand she had lost all her security by selling her home, so I was trying to reassure her it would be ok. I said to her many times, "Just trust in me and have a little faith."

I was going nowhere. I had found her.

But deep down, I knew she still felt vulnerable, with no home to call her own, no job, and having left her three children.

She was a mum of three.

She loved her 'chicks,' as she called them. She was a caregiver, not just to them but to all of us.

I never said it, but I wanted it and felt it. I wanted her family to become my family.

She was going to miss them when she moved. I had started trying to help her daughter with her business as a 'coach.' The two sons told her to get on with her own life and not to worry.

Kerry put her kids first, so it was always going to be in the back of her mind that she would be so far away from them. She also had a grandson who she doted on and loved spending time with. She was going to miss him a lot, but again, we had a plan and a budget for her to go back and forth at any time to see them.

I should have seen it.

I should have slowed down.

I should have understood her fears much better.

I should have just stayed in England.

She might have left me sooner!

We both had unspoken issues.

I did not realise it in her straight away, but I could always feel something dark and distant in her. I would often put my hand on her heart and ask if she was ok. (Now, I think it was probably only making her fears worse.)

It was not until I was alone that I realised we both had insecurities. We both needed some help.

She told me she got scared in relationships after her marriage ended. Her other relationships with men seemed to end in bad ways.

It seemed when she got close to someone, the idea of losing her space, feeling like she was losing her independence, feeling vulnerable, or trusting people got the better of her, and eventually, she would just run away. Or it might have been just me she ran from!

I was going nowhere. I loved her. I think I must have put too much pressure on her, but not knowingly. Maybe she feared being hurt all over again.

I should have held on tighter or just let her be free.

But sometimes, fear and ADHD got in my way.

I must have been making some bad decisions, taking things for granted, and not taking enough time to reassure her. I was trying, but obviously, in the wrong way.

CHAPTER 10

Something Changed

I came home after eleven months.

I was alone there; only seeing Kerry every five weeks or so was just not enough. I cannot explain how much I hated it. I really hated it. If I had the balls, I would have come home much sooner. I missed her so much, and in some respects, we should have really started our relationship when I came home. Not when I was 4000 miles away.

I was still finding out about her. From the bits I had seen, I could see a lovely future. We were getting on fine.

She was a beautiful soul but with deep hurt inside. She hid it very well most of the time.

Some days felt endless on the island, and I was always waiting for her next visit or next call.

Our plans were still in place. I was getting the house ready for her to come over, with a bed for her grandson, ceiling fans in all the bedrooms, and even air conditioning.

I was building our new home, but of course, without the female touches. That would have been her job!

I do not think it was ever going to be our forever home, just home, until we decided what was next. In my mind, it was a beautiful place to start something special.

In my mind, I was building our future.

I do not think I was ever paying enough attention to what she needed or wanted. I was just charging along at top speed, trying to make things happen as usual, taking things for granted and not listening.

Christmas came.

I had a video call from her. It was great to see all her family around the table and eating lovely food in our home.

I had made myself a Christmas dinner, but it is not the same on your own.

I spoke to them all. It was the first time I had chatted with her oldest son. He was a good-looking man, and he seemed to like me. He was a nice bloke, and his girlfriend was very pretty. I wish we had chatted more. I had met the other son and the daughter before. I had taken them all out for a meal when I was last home.

Anthony and his partner came; it was so nice to have my family together. It was great to see them all opening their presents.

I had made sure I had gotten them all something as a gift, and of course, I made sure Kerry had some special gifts–her favourite perfume and an iPad. She only had her 'phone to look at,' so I thought a larger screen would be much better than just a phone.

I hoped she liked them.

She had left my gifts and two books with me on her last trip out, so I had something to open, too.

Even her brother and his wife were there. I spoke to his wife for a while. She was a nice lady, very chatty, and had lovely hair. She wanted to know all about me and loved our home.

I felt I had been accepted into the family. Everyone was there except me! I was living my Christmas through a video screen. I did not want the call to end, but as usual, I did not want to get in the way of their day.

I did not want to somehow spoil it.

They all stayed at our home for a few days, so I know they had an enjoyable time and lots of great food.

We still chatted every day. Thank God for WhatsApp.

New Year's Day came, and I was a bit down. I must admit I was missing her very much. Christmas time is quite emotional, and the fact I was not there made it worse. I felt totally empty after that call, but I knew I would be home soon.

As soon as I could get my dog booked on a plane, I came home. As silly as it sounds, I used to watch the airplanes take off. The airport was alongside the dog-walking beach. I found it strange that my first thought when a plane took off was that *'they're leaving…?'*

What is wrong with me?

I was coming home back to England to get our relationship back on course. We both said we needed to be riding a 'tandem bike,' so we were both going in the same direction.

I wanted to reassure her that she was all I wanted and needed. I hoped she felt the same.

I would not let her down ever.

I had no plan to return abroad; my only plan was to be with her and try to build something real. i came home to be with her, nothing more, nothing less.

On my way home in the taxi, she sent me a text message.

The text read, *'I LOVE YOU.'*

She had been busy cooking for us. Batch cooking, she called it, so we could eat lots of delicious food together. It was delicious; it always was. I had gotten used to eating anything with ham and cheese!

The first day home was lovely. It was a bit strange to be in the UK, but equally lovely to be home.

We walked the dogs, had breakfast, played Monopoly, and watched some movies. Everything felt normal again after a few quiet moments.

It was lovely to share the bed with her again. I love that I could make her feel good. We cuddled. It was so nice to be in bed with her again. We hugged and kissed.

It was so good to be home with her after so long.

Then, on the second day, she went quiet.

I asked if she was okay. I could always feel her. I asked her what was wrong.

We were in the bedroom.

She broke down in tears. I had never seen anyone cry like that before.

She told me something from her past—something she had carried for years. She was still blaming herself. She still held it in. She said she was not worthy of anything nice in her life and that it was all her fault.

I hugged her until I could calm her down. I kept saying, "It was not your fault."

I was shocked, but it instantly explained a lot of her behaviour towards me and our relationship—the fact that she found it hard, almost impossible, to trust.

I was honoured that she eventually told me and seemed, at that moment, to trust me completely.

Later that day, we managed to get back to some normality. We played Monopoly again, had fun, ate nice food, had just general chit chat, cuddled on the sofa, and watched TV. Just normal stuff.

That night, I tickled her back to soothe her. You know, drawing letters or numbers on her back? She had to guess the letters. I was just trying to let her know I was there for her, to reassure and comfort her.

And then she said something that hit me deeper than anything ever had. She said, "Thank you for not giving up on me."

It was the most profound thing anyone has ever said to me–ever.

I wanted to marry her then. I still do. I even had a ring ready. I wanted us to have a home together; I still do. We even talked about that.

But I never had the courage to ask her, just in case she said no.

I should have asked again—how thoughtless was I?

I was just nervous that she would say no.

I do not think I gave our love the time to flourish. I was always doubting myself, always in a hurry. That's where my childhood behaviours and ADHD were kicking in, always thinking I would be rejected, that I was not good enough. It was my normal, ingrained beliefs.

I am always second-guessing myself, never stopping, not just giving anything enough time.

She needed to know she was safe with me. And I needed to know I was enough for her.

Maybe if we had both healed a little more, it might have been different. I know we could have had something utterly amazing if we were not both hiding our fears, giving ourselves time, and being more honest with each other.

Perhaps I was just too boring for her!

CHAPTER 11

The Third Day

Monday morning started like any other. I made her a cup of tea in bed. Then an hour or so later, all hell broke loose.

She was *leaving*–going and not coming back.

By 11 o'clock, she had packed her things and left. I was in total shock, another massive U-turn.

That morning, we had planned to get a new bathroom sorted out. I had taken the dog for a walk. When I got home, she had packed all her stuff into her car.

I asked, "What's going on?"

In a blur, she said someone had seen a post on Facebook, my Facebook page.

Someone had commented on my post about how long I was home, and I stupidly replied to them, *'I don't know, but not for long, I hope.'*

One of the family told her I could not be trusted. That was all that was needed, the final nail in my coffin.

What I meant to say was that I hoped I was not back for long because Kerry and I had made plans to either go back abroad and try out island life or buy our own home in England so we could start in our own shared home.

We had looked at some houses weeks before on the Internet. She wanted to be able to see the sea, and I wanted a bit of space to do stuff. We had talked about doing a food stall, not for the money, just for fun—something we could do together. Of course, she could cook anything, so it was going to be a success.

So, in reality, I had no idea how long we were going to be in the UK.

I thought it was our business, not anyone else's. Again, I was very wrong. Just shows how a text can be misconstrued. I must have been thoughtless in my words, but it was our private conversation, I thought. No one else knew about our plans.

However, I paid the price again and lost another relationship.

I had no time to talk about anything much; I had only been home three short days!

She told me I was charismatic.

I said thank you. I did not know if it was a compliment or not. *I'm not sure what charismatic is.*

When she left, she said she was overwhelmed by everything. When I look back now, she was going to leave, anyway, no matter what I did or said.

Definitely another man involved! She was sending and receiving a lot of texts, so I'm sure a bigger, better distraction was waiting for her.

I am not that stupid.

Maybe just the sight of me home was enough to make her run!

What did I do wrong?

Were my hopes and dreams too big?

I always told her to have faith in me, to have faith in us, and that I was going nowhere. I was here to support, care, and love her.

I think she just got frightened of commitment or had found someone new. I will never know that either. Maybe she didn't love me at all. Maybe I was just wasting my breath. I might say the wrong thing sometimes, but I'm a solid guy.

I had never knowingly hurt her or let her down.

I am still deeply in love with her.

I often wondered if she was with someone else. That would have explained all the text she was getting—after all, she craved love. I do not think she knew or cared how much turmoil, heartache, and chaos she left behind.

CHAPTER 12

Our Word

I loved getting close to her. It is such a basic thing to do in a relationship. We had a special word: *tingle!*

I hope it was our word, not the word that *every* guy got…if you understand.

I hope I helped her with her sadness. At least in the end, she trusted me enough to tell me something no one else would ever know, at least not from my lips.

I hope she felt the care in me that I had for her.

I hope she never forgets me. I hope she will come home…

I really hope.

I do believe in second chances. I believe if I put it out into the universe, they will be listening to me. So far, I have had no reply!

I believe anything and everything is possible. I always told her, "I am going nowhere." I was here for her, and I was worth her trust and love.

I am so stupid to have let this once-in-a-lifetime connection slip through my fingers. It was not a perfect relationship, but whose relationship is? To me, it was not far off being perfect. I know it takes two to have a relationship, but I've unfortunately learned a hard lesson.

Couples need to talk about everything, be honest, and tell their secrets. It was my fault that I set no boundaries. I did not know how or why. Why did no one give me that bit of advice when I was younger? I wish someone had.

This might sound like just a breakup story, and I need to grow a pair of balls, but for how my brain works, it was like I had been cut in half. When she walked out the door, her last words to me were, "I do not want a relationship. I am not good with relationships," and she just went.

She ran away.

Unfortunately for me, I am confident she had already started another relationship.

Life can be unfair and cruel. Did I deserve it all? All I can hope for now is that, at least in time, we can become friendly.

I've managed over the years to still be on friendly terms with both of my ex wives. I know that with another man around, it's not going to happen.

Now when I look back, this was mostly my fault. Trying to have a relationship when living so far apart.

I forgot to do so many things and did not notice the signs. How could I give someone else security if I doubted my own? I could do all the things I was supposed to do and needed to do. But I just forgot! Not on purpose, I just did. Sometimes, I forgot to hold her hand. I forgot to tell her how much I cared. I forgot so many trivial things. So, with all my sadness, it was probably my fault all along.

CHAPTER 13

Moving Forward

I am taking therapy. I started a week ago. It was strange to open my heart to a stranger, but I felt better afterwards.

I tried Reiki. Guess what? My chakras were blocked. My heart was the wrong colour!

I was a mess in my head. Therapy is helping me understand myself so much better. So is the Internet and hypnosis, and now I have even learnt how to manifest.

I am much calmer in my thoughts; I have quietened my mind. I am finding out so many things about me that honestly, I was not aware of. I am starting to feel better. A better stronger person again.

I am going to be the best version of me. I am now manifesting each morning, and all the good things are coming back into my life again.

I am working again, cutting hair. I have updated my home and car. Life is getting back to normal, but I do not have my friend, Kerry.

I miss my friend very much.

CHAPTER 14

The Journey

I was never into the 'journey.' For me, it was always about the destination. My journey, which has taken me sixty-four years to realise that I needed to go on, has started.

I always said I hated the 'journey' because I just wanted to be at the destination.

I can see how wrong I was. It is all about the journey.

I need to learn to take the time to enjoy everything. They say it is never too late to learn.

I deeply love Kerry like no one before. I do not really know why, but I do.

I think I always will, but I know it is time to let her out of my thoughts and let her go and be free.

I hope sometimes she thinks about us and has nice memories of me now and then.

I tried, but obviously not hard enough. I have learnt a hard lesson.

Now, I need to learn to be happy with myself again and feel my own worth.

I need boundaries, forget trying to be perfect for someone else, not trying to please other people at my own expense, knowing that I am good enough as I am.

I now must start believing in myself again, my new future. I know I will attract love back into my life. I am just not ready yet!

I am now on my way to a new beginning, on my own, having to start all over again. It's terrifying at my age, but I know I can do it. I am so grateful and blessed to have the love and support of my friends.

While I walk my dog, I often wonder what she is doing. *Did she ever love me? Did she ever really like me? Will she ever remember me*? As silly as it sounds, it is especially important.

She left me, and there has not been any contact, nothing. It's as if I never existed.

I wanted to count for something, something special in her life. Anything. She just left so fast with no explanation. That is what hurts the most. It is so brutal.

I am putting this out into the universe so she can feel me. I am not complete yet, but I will be. Then, hopefully, we will find each other again.

Faith is something that cannot be seen. You must believe. I believed in her and our dreams.

Maybe we were never meant to be! Maybe she told me, and I was just not listening. All I know is she is and was a very special lady. I so wish it could have ended in a vastly different way.

So now, I have had no contact, just avoidance from her side. To this day, she has never contacted me. It is awful, and it still hurts. I still do not understand what went wrong.

I must have been an unbelievably bad person in an earlier life to get this reaction. Perhaps I am just not that lovable.

I have learnt that it is not up to me to try to make someone else happy; it is up to them. My conclusion is that there was nothing I could have done to save our relationship.

I presume if it were real love, we would have worked through the problems—or at least tried.

It seems as though Kerry just needed to have her space and independence—*to hell with anyone else.*

I am very grateful, at least I spent some good times with her. I wish she would hold my hand again.

My final wish is that someday, somehow, she will say sorry for how she treated me; at least then, I will understand why and where I went so wrong, and then I can truly move on.

The inspiration for this story came from a song by *U2*. It goes something like this:

'You got a face not spoiled by beauty
I have some scars from where I've been
You've got eyes that can see right through me
You're not afraid of anything they've seen

I was told that I would feel nothing the first time
I don't know how these cuts heal
But in you I found a rhyme

If there is a light you can't always see
And there is a world we can't always be
If there is a dark that we shouldn't doubt
And there is a light, don't let it go out'

Words by Bono,

'Song for Someone.'

Kerry.

Do not ever let your light go out.

I leave you the best of myself.

Untill next time!

POETRY

Stars in the Sky

Like a star in the sky, the lights of the big
birds keep coming
bringing holidaymakers from across the
globe
it's calm, it's warm, it's everything you could
wish for
apart from your partner, who is not there
this is a paradise island with the people you
love,
but an endless day without them
I see walkers, swimmers, runners—you name
it
all out, enjoying the warmth of the sun
it's a chance to forget
a chance to see the world with different eyes
a chance to regroup

a chance to live a new life
but without your soul mate, it's hell
making friends in 2025 is difficult at the best
of times, with people's heads buried in their
phones
I long to see my friend.
I just wish we had a similar dream

Today

Today is our magnificent gift…
Use it to change your world
use it to change somebody else's
use it to become the person you really want
to be
use it to make all your dreams come true
use it to begin again
use it to be you again
use it to shine your light bright

No Tomorrow

There is no tomorrow
tomorrow never comes
it exists only in our imagination
the only purpose is to help us decide what to
do today
what could the future 'today' look like
if we didn't take it for granted?

You

I want you
I want you now, now in my arms
to hold you, to hold you, so you know you're
held
I want you
I want you beside me, warm, our love
growing
to grow, to live, to share
Kerry, I want you
I want you to catch your breath
I want to breathe you in
I want you to have faith
I want to hold you, to hold you more and
more
to hold you tight, never letting you go
I want you to have faith in me
I want us
forever.

Control

It's strange
we all like a bit of control
sometimes, people we let into our lives take
over
we love
we worry
we try not to disappoint
we try to please
we get lost in something, someone else
sometimes, it's great, but also not
I have lost control
bending my rules for someone else,
losing control
that's what love can do.

Watching 7

It's raining
my dog has had a swim in the sea
she's happy
now, we both watch the world go by,
sipping my coffee and ham and cheese
toasty in the rain
at our favorite beach cafe in Playa Honda
even the waiter brings her a bowl of water
she's now on my lap, wet and cuddling into
me
I like it
people always laugh
when they see her curled up with her dad
we have a bond
I know she loves me without a question
she was given to me from heaven
but really, from the vet
I met 7 when she was a baby
with a broken leg
I rescued her
like all springers, as happy as can be,
always with a ball in her mouth

Don't Let The Light Go Out

I just wish she could talk
I often think about a dog's wisdom
I wonder what it would be like!
I think she just loves,
the walks, being with me, and of course, her
ball
she never takes her eyes off me,
not for a moment
what would I do without her?
Thank you, 7, for always being there
I hope you loved the walks and my nonstop
talking
she's still wet and curled up on my lap,
I cannot think of anything nicer
the rain is now dripping down my neck,
time to move,
she is still tucked in
my coffee is cold
now, she will have to listen to me all the way
home
and, of course, she has her ball
my day with 7

Magic Mask

I have a mask that does not often come off
now that I have retired, the mask does not
work
I am invisible!
I have no credibility!
I have little purpose!
No one needs me
I have hobbies of a sort–
karting
it makes my heart beat
I take photos,
trying to find colours that I wish were in my
life
all my pictures are full of colour, full of sound
that is the world I see
it's what I want it to be

Music

Some tunes move me;
some words make me cry;
some words lift me up
I think how I could change the world?
music says what I only wish I could say
with my mask, I could not fail
with my mask, I could make a difference
but now my magic mask is nearly worn off
I am trying to find where I fit in
am I liked?
am I loved?
does anybody want me?
the real me?
I'm sure we all have our own masks
without my mask, I'm lost
I had it for so many years
I need to find a new mask!

Intimacy

Intimacy is not who you let touch you.
intimacy is who you text at 3 am
intimacy is giving someone your attention,
when ten other people are asking for it
intimacy is that person who's always on your
mind,
no matter how distracted you are
intimacy is for the one your world stops for

OTHER BOOKS BY THE AUTHOR:

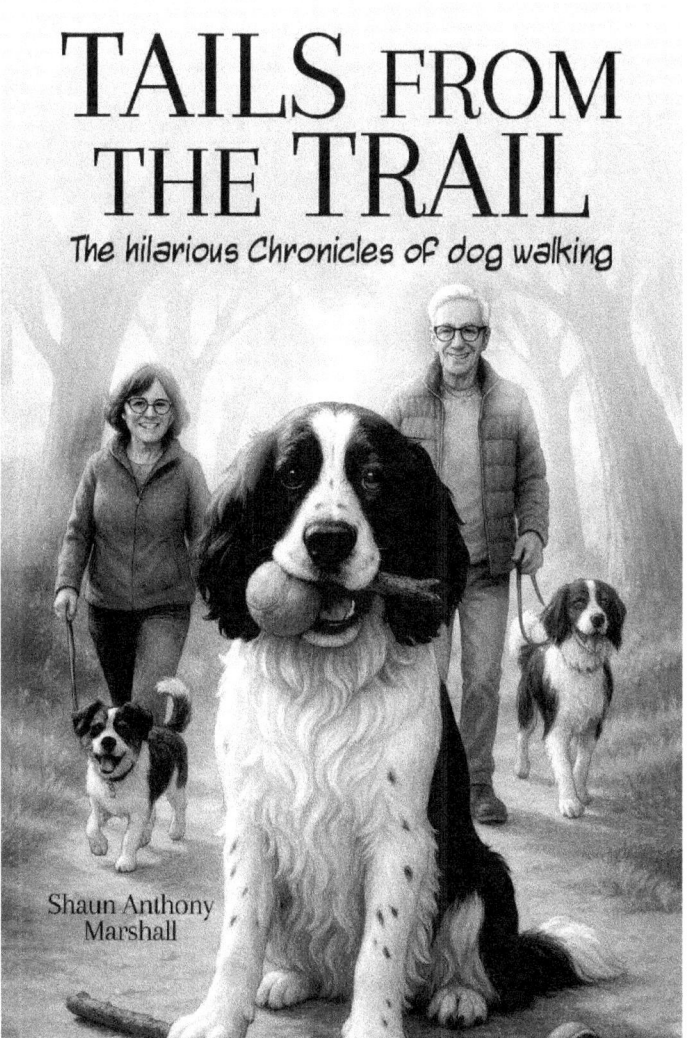